Chasing Light

A Collection of Poems

Patricia Glinton-Meicholas

CHASING LIGHT is Patricia Glinton-Meicholas's third book of poetry and a finalist for the International Proverse Prize 2012. A challenging and controversial complexity of opinion pervades the collection, accurately signaled by the double-entendre of the title. Taken as a whole, the poems express concern for humankind worldwide, with a particular emphasis on the life of women, particularly those with an African or Caribbean heritage. Glinton-Meicholas speaks equally for those she imagines to live colourless, passionless lives and those whose private relations are ample and fulfilling. She responds to regional and international events, particularly the troubles brought by local politics and attitudes, and by war. The poems show a person passionately aware and caring, conscious of deity in various manifestations and hoping for the world's salvation from this source. Nevertheless she acknowledges that man has free-will and that it is for man to exercise his free-will to solve or avoid problems. The writing – with occasional lines in creole – is sophisticated and rewards close attention from the reader.

Bahamian-born **PATRICIA GLINTON-MEICHOLAS**, writer, editor, cultural critic and academic, is an honours graduate of the University of the West Indies and the University of Miami. Recognized nationally for her contributions to Bahamian literature, she was first winner of the Bahamas Cacique Award for Writing (1995) and recipient of a Silver Jubilee of Independence Medal for Literature (1998). She was the first woman to present the prestigious Sir Lynden Pindling Memorial Lecture (Nassau, 2005). Her books include *An Evening in Guanima* (short stories based on Bahamian folktale motifs), the novel, *A Shift in the Light*, and two volumes of poetry (*No Vacancy in Paradise* and *Robin's Song*). She co-wrote *Bahamian Art 1492 to 1992* and contributed to the *Macmillan Dictionary of Art*. Her story 'The Gaulin Wife' appears in the Penguin anthology *Under the Storyteller's Spell* (1988). A monograph on Bahamian folktales was published in the Encuentros series of the Inter-American Development Bank Cultural Centre. Her most recent book is *Years of Favour*, a 264-page history and pictorial of the Roman Catholic Archdiocese of The Bahamas 1960-2010 (with P. Neko Meicholas and Carla Glinton). She has also written and directed several historical documentaries for television.

Chasing Light

A Collection of Poems

Patricia Glinton-Meicholas

Proverse Hong Kong

Chasing Light
by Patricia Glinton-Meicholas.
3d edition published in Hong Kong by Proverse Hong Kong,
June 2017.

ISBN: 978-988-8228-11-9
Available from: https://www.createspace.com/7250959

1st edition published in paperback in Hong Kong by Proverse Hong Kong,
19 November 2013.

ISBN 978-988-8227-18-1

1st edition distribution (Hong Kong and worldwide):
The Chinese University Press of Hong Kong,
The Chinese University of Hong Kong, Shatin,
New Territories, Hong Kong, SAR. E-mail: cup@cuhk.edu.hk
Web site: www.chineseupress.com

1st edition distribution (United Kingdom):
Christine Penney, Stratford-upon-Avon, Warwickshire CV37 6DN,
England. Email: chrisp@proversepublishing.com
Distribution enquiries: Proverse Hong Kong, P. O. Box 259, Tung Chung
Post Office, Tung Chung, Lantau Island, NT, Hong Kong SAR, China.
E-mail: proverse@netvigator.com
Web site: www.proversepublishing.com

Cover image by P. Neko Meicholas.
Cover design by P. Neko Meicholas and Artist Hong Kong Com.

British Library Cataloguing in Publication Data.
A catalogue record for this book is available
from the British Library.

Acknowledgement

Profound thanks to
His Excellency Sir Arthur Foulkes, GVCO, LLD,
for contributing the Preface.

Acknowledgements and Previous Publication Credits

'A Witch's Tale'. Earlier version published in *Womanspeak*, Vol. 6, Nassau, Bahamas, 2012, pp. 42-43.
'Banishing Grief'. Substantially different version, 'Junkanoo Heaven: for Jackson Logan Burnside, III', published in *Yinna: the Journal of the Bahamas Association for Cultural Studies*, Vol. 4, 2012, pp. 158-161 (pbk). Bahamas Association for Cultural Studies (BACUS) in association with Guanima Press. Nassau, Bahamas.
'Baptism'. Earlier version '2030' published in *Yinna: the Journal of the Bahamas Association for Cultural Studies*, Vol. 1, 2000, pp. 123-128. BACUS in association with Guanima Press. Nassau, Bahamas.
'Bent Light'. Earlier version published in *Yinna: the Journal of the Bahamas Association for Cultural Studies*, Vol. 3, June 2011, p. 114-116. BACUS in association with Guanima Press, Nassau, Bahamas.
'Conversation with God'. Previously published in *Poui: Cave Hill Journal of Creative Writing*, No. 10, December 2009, pp. 54-55 (pbk).
'I Want to Go Caribbean'. Earlier version published in *An Anthology of Caribbean Poetry for Carifesta X*, August 2008, pp. 12-13, 2008 (pbk). Published by Ministry of Culture, Youth & Sport, Georgetown, Guyana.
'Letter to the Editor of Walls and Public Billboards'. Substantially different version published as 'Message from on High' in *Poui: Cave Hill Journal of Creative Writing,* No. 11, December 2010, pp. 30-31. Department of Language, Linguistics & Literature, Univ. of the West Indies, Cave Hill Campus, Barbados, W.I.

'On the Effects of a Note Played by Wynton Marsalis'. Originally published in *No Vacancy in Paradise*, Guanima Press, 2001. Republished Sunday, 2 May 2010 at 12:01am in online journal "tongues of the ocean". http://tonguesoftheocean.org/2010/05/on-the-effects-of-a-note-played-by-wynton-marsalis/.

'Prayer for Our Sister Haiti'. Substantially different version published in *Across Borders: the Work Issue: an international literary journal*, Lebanon College Press, 15 Hanover Street, Lebanon, N.H., USA, 2010, pp. 83-85.

'Predation'. Previously published as 'Predation I' in *Anthurium: A Caribbean Studies Journal*: Vol. 8: Issue 1, Article 12, 2011. Online: Available at: http://scholarlyrepository.miami.edu/anthurium/vol8/iss1/12.

'Predation II'. *Anthurium: A Caribbean Studies Journal*: Vol. 8: Issue 1, Article 13, 2011. Online: Available at: http://scholarlyrepository.miami.edu/anthurium/vol8/iss1/13.

'Rage Comes'. Substantially different version published as 'Rage' in *Poui: Cave Hill Journal of Creative Writing*, No. 11, December 2010, pp. 29-30.

'Solace'. First published in *Yinna: the Journal of the Bahamas Association for Cultural Studies*, Vol. 2, 2007, pp. 146-147. Produced by BACUS in association with Guanima Press, Nassau, Bahamas. Republished in *Across Borders: the Work Issue: an international literary journal*, Lebanon College Press, 15 Hanover Street, Lebanon, N.H., USA, 2010, pp.15-16.

'To Our Mothers on Fathers' Day'. Published in part in *Poui: Cave Hill Journal of Creative Writing,* No. 10, December 2009, p. 38. Department of Language, Linguistics & Literature, Univ. of the West Indies, Cave Hill Campus, Barbados, W.I.

COVER IMAGE
P. Neko Meicholas

Preface
by Sir Arthur Foulkes

Chasing light is akin to trying to contain in one's hands water scooped from an ocean or a river. It is always a partial and fleeting experience. Yet we keep on trying. Our attempts, no matter their limited satisfaction and reward, are just as often exhilarating and ever enticing.

Just as life is suffused with mysteries that sometimes yield a little to the quest for enlightenment, but are never fully knowable, in chasing light we but experience glimpses of meaning and glimmers of the ineffable.

Light surprises and beckons to us in shadows and in reflections, in eclipses and in rainbows. So diminished is the light at times that it is only perceived through hope and the imagination. So brilliant is the light at times that we require filters lest we are overwhelmed or blinded.

Poetry is a fount of the imagination and a filter that helps us to chase the light and to grasp it just long enough for us to capture some of its essence even as it scatters off with us in eternal pursuit.

In *Chasing Light*, a kaleidoscope of musings in varied tones, Patricia Glinton-Meicholas aids our eternal quest. She is ideally suited to so do. For her, identity is not a simplistic matter answered in either/or propositions. It is an ongoing discovery understood best in the language of paradox and poetry.

As a writer, editor, cultural critic and academic, she evinces a cosmopolitan worldview, blending a global consciousness with a Caribbean and Bahamian spirit deeply influenced by her

African roots. Her dedication to the fuller liberation and well-being of women is urgent and passionate.

Glinton-Meicholas's poetry is regional and indigenous, but also universal. In 'These Few Words' she offers a love song. In 'Bent Light' and other poems there is a mystical poignancy. She rails at injustice and hypocrisy. Yet there is also hope in abundance and the possibility of salvation.

'Prayer for Our Sister Haiti' and 'I Want to go Caribbean' embrace the Caribbean civilization in which Glinton-Meicholas is as at home as a West Indian and Bahamian daughter and poet.

She can barely contain the beauty and the light that bursts from her rhapsodic imagination in poems such as 'Today'...

> "Today, I'll unfold like morning,
> lifting my face to sunlight
> like waking mimosa and tamarind leaves.
> I'll chase beauty, hunting in her countless
> haunts,
> scent the must of her perfume in petrichor,
> spy her green fire in the emerald flash
> of a hummingbird's jeweled breast,
> capture her prism in a rain-blanched sky,
> toast her spirit in the burgundy of sunset."

The art of writing in The Bahamas, whether novels, essays, short stories, poetry or other literary expression, has tended to lag behind the visual arts. This is beginning to change.

The canon of Bahamian literature is growing appreciably thanks to the fine contributions of intrepid spirits like Glinton-Meicholas, whose writings and teaching are inspiring a new generation of writers and poets.

It has been my privilege as a journalist and as a politician over many decades to have tried my hand at the writing craft. I have also observed the art and practice of language at home and abroad over these many years.

I must admit some distress at how poorly English is often understood and used. So, it is with considerable enthusiasm that I celebrate and recommend *Chasing Light*. Patricia Glinton-Meicholas masters and revels in the language, employing it with finesse and grace, exuberantly and meticulously.

I am proud of her as both a fellow Bahamian and an occasional practitioner of the writer's art. Glinton-Meicholas thrills us with the hope of what is yet to arise from her imagination and from her influence on a new generation of Bahamian authors.

Arthur A. Foulkes, GCMG, LLD
Governor General
Commonwealth of The Bahamas

20 September, 2013
Nassau, Bahamas

Chasing Light
Table of Contents

CHASING SHADOW

Prayer for Our Sister Haiti

Lord Almighty, the God I know,
send a dry, dry season to Haiti!
Let there be long droughts
of hatred, rape and death.
Dam the river of sanctioned misery,
cap the flow
flooding from ancient inhumanity.
Let chaos and calamity reign no more.
Waterless, let thirsty sprouts
of neocolonial ambition,
lush green fields
of greed and strife
die, leaving no seed
to spring, entangle,
strangle beloved Ayiti[1] anew.
Your daughter is waiting;
she is stumbling, let her not fall.

Mami Wata,[2] send floods on dry Haiti –
mighty rivers of grace and goodness,
wine of charity to fill, overflow
dry chalices of stony hearts;
fast streams of forbearance,
breaking barriers of class and calumny,
breeching ancient bulwarks
of race and riches
that forge and guard the fastnesses
of exclusion.
Send relief…
In racing tides of wisdom,
wash away ignorance,
quench throat-burning, mind-corroding
anger and grief.
Papa nou ki nan siѐl la,[3]

time's long past
for reviewing your register,
for writing Haiti's name
into the contract,
into the sanctuary
of your saving grace.
Time to transcend the past,
descend
before our sister falls,
drowns in the gulf
of gifts with codicils
of apocrypha of aid
and prize-winning tales
of Christian charity.

Time, Lord, to walk Haiti's streets again,
letting the hem of your garments
staunch the issue of blood
in quiet miracle once more....
Your daughter's children are waiting;
they hunger;
spread a table before them.

You brazen gods of cheap alloy,
you lords of earthly power and coin;
open ears long stopped
by devious doctrine,
treacherous treaty and corollary,
by rapine wrapped in claim of reparation,
hear our sister's cry!
This daughter of your covert lust
thirsts and shakes from infection,
borne in the bite of your rabid greed.
Save her!
Let fragile tents of survival
beget deep-rooted shelter,
strongholds and fortresses

of resilient freedom.
Let them flourish to cover fields
of torn flesh, razor-sharp shards
of broken dreams.

La Sirène,[4] blue-garbed and beautiful,
trouble the waters of l'Artibonite,[5]
birth the balm of a New World Bethesda.
Earth Mother, let the blood you spilled,
swilled drunkenly on the fated day,
pay the price of binding up,
healing our sister's riven breast.
Loa[6] or Holy Spirit of life,
let Haiti live!
Reanimate loins, swell wombs
long barren of optimism.
Let them give birth,
in fat-cheeked, smiling multiples,
to redeemed and unquenchable
new life, new faith, new hope.

You Lords of Coyaba[7] and trembling earth,
hasten the day of grace!
Your daughter is waiting,
her children are waiting,
the world's children are waiting….
Soon, soon, soon, soon,
they will wait no more.

Bent Light

My friend bent light.
His heart was radiant,
dyed deep in the generosity of red,
shimmering with blue of hopeful sky,
pink with the passion of flamingo's wing,
painting rainbows
on clouded firmaments of despair.

He loved
this illuminated soul,
condemned though he was
by bargain-basement apostles
who see the beam
between heaven and humanity
as straight, hard
monochrome.

Self-satisfied saviours
retooled gospels,
inscribed footnotes,
took to television
to lend credence, codify
the deep dye of his sins.
They revealed him, kneeled him,
keel-hauled him beneath
the ponderous ship of Zion.
Holy precincts
rang with fervent hallelujahs
when this golden boy,
knees worn out at the mourner's bench,
confessed.

Said they healed him,
straightened the bend,
re-gendered him –
the iron maiden of their righteousness
smugly slicing away
parts spilling from its vicious confines.
His joy, his verve,
embrace of all who didn't fit,
were felled
by the corroded, toxic axe
of salvation.

They do not know,
as he didn't know,
our Creator is
First Bender of Light,
Sire of the Platypus,
High Lord of Refraction,
the God, whose prismatic will
split the womb of our mother blackness
with fiery crystal seed,
fathering his rainbow children.

By thy refractive grace,
lighten their darkness,
O Trichromatic Lord!
Save us from the wrath
of soul-thirsty angels,
whose fangs ache to suck joy
from the veins of strays,
whose splayed feet
cannot hold to the third rail
of Pharisee mercy.

Show these saints that love and mercy
are many-gendered things,
and their tight white beam
is but an imprisoned ray,
offspring of your infinite light
awash with jewels of rainbows denied.

Single Motherhood

You stand so serene, so beautiful
an exclamation of peace
in the crazed sentence of the world.
A pregnant sentience shines
from downcast eyes and ageless cheeks;
your words hang on the threshold
of sound, your robe almost floats…
fancy giving scent to a rumour of roses
in wild sage sweet hush of morning air.

Enfolded in the eternal quietude
of your seaside meditation,
do you recall the rupture of your girlhood,
when divinity chose you as vessel
in which to plant its redemptive seed?
Does your sisters' chill fright grip your heart
when cold science –
prosaic locum for winged herald –
announces impending motherhood?

Do you mourn for your distant echoes
when fear cries denial,
when souls almost devoid of faith...
when modern tongues
– lacking the proper idiom –
give voice to doom
in place of magnificat?
Or when their Josephs
– pale shadows of yours –
make solo, graceless hegiras,
abandoning your sisters
to seek their own accommodation?

Does your heart bleed for their children,

who will bear the weight of crosses
with scant chance of kingship,
dismal promise of a throne?

No, the weathered nacre of your lips
has perfected pudicity and silence,
smiling the same
amid our pitiful joys and sorrows.
The sun cannot reach your heart
to thaw its secrets
or admit frantic supplication.

Your shoulders will bear no greater load
than the weight of transient birds;
your head, no more than a crown
of monarchs.

So, you stand untouched, unaggrieved
still, when sister wombs learn rudely of life
– harsh, unwelcome lessons –
cancelling cotillions,
quashing quinceañeras and virginal debut,
leaving the future devoid of aves.

Departure

For Patricia Louise

And now she's gone,
shedding her heavy skin
of days, months, years
of east, west, north and south
of past and present
of limiting circumference and dimension;
her compass now calibrated
only to futurity and infinite space,
orienting her flight
by stars and galaxies,
sloughing off the weight of history
and the rude minutiae
of metered life.

Left suddenly behind
with no time for adjustment,
disconsolate nature mourned her,
pouring out lamentations
in rivulets of rain,
shrilling her anger
in the shrieks of gulls,
pleading in casuarina sighs,
pouring out her pain
in howl of wind
in the sobbing of the sea
in dank, drowned coves;
finally signaling drear acceptance
in the pall of blackbirds
covering the hearse of earth
that bore her child into eternity.

Yet, none of her abysses
that rend earth's mass to molten core
can plunge deeper
than the lover's frantic search
for threads of memory
to stitch up raw wounds
of loss,
when ardent flesh has been ripped,
divorced forever
from answering flesh.

And surely, nature knows no grief
like the sundered heart,
forced to pen a fervent and fragrant life
on a limp and scentless page;
or – more grievous still –
to hymn – back straight,
lips trembling,
dignity held by tattered thread –
the drear, comfortless words
of our beloved's funeral dirge.

To Our Mothers on Fathers' Day

Our dear mothers
who art in heaven,
how high you have risen!
Hallowed be the name
of the One who lifted you up
from scrub-floor knees,
raptured washboard hands,
to be raised in the zealous
unending praise of rescued refugees!

It was you, coconut-husk women,
who drew us to the still waters
of your loving breasts,
sheltering us
from the raging tides
of marital mismatch,
which splintered the quiet seascape
of your treasured young girls' lives.

Yea, though you walked through dark valleys
of starless, two-job, car-less nights,
you feared no evil, save the spectre
of homeless, hungry children.
Then, the sainted fount of your maternity
would spring again,
well up in you, propel you
when stiff joints, tired feet and fresh despair
threatened to stall you –
All for us.

You spread tables of plenty before us
in the presence of penury
and neighbours
who fed and spread tales
of hush funds and errant flesh
cheating of credit;
your straw-plaiting
cassava-digging
crab-catching
coconut-grating
nail-chipped, never idle hands,
whose beauty your calluses crowned.

We have found goodness and mercy
dwelling in the house of love,
built from the crushing beams
of the cross you bore for us
with silk cotton courage,
lignum vitae loins,
to the bitter calvaries
of lonely women.
So, on each festive Fathers' Day,
Yemaya Mama, Our Lady of Waters,
Nana of our tears,[8]
hallow and bless their names –
our coral-bowelled mothers,
who fearlessly fathered us.

Banishing Grief

How I wish
these omnipresent
importunate beings,
these purloiners of our peace,
these thieves of light,
had been brought to heel;
put on a stop list,
assigned an expiration date,
marked for obsolescence.
How I wish, they had never been born
to hound and bedevil humankind,
but had been left to languish, calcify
in the cold and cavernous womb of time.

But here they are again,
grim shadows at our doors,
instruments of pain in hand,
speaking agony in a babel of tongues;
set to lay siege,
form a phalanx of misery,
hurl burning embers at our hearts,
block roads to forces of rescue,
choke avenues to joy.

The crass interlopers will fight for –
insist upon –
extended, soul-reaming stays;
shuttering windows,
shutting out light
banishing sleep,
exacting keening;

forcing us to howl at the melancholic moon
like beasts, feral and maddened,
wracking the bowels of midnight.

But this I know…
Light will come again,
demanding entrance;
forcing its way
through needle-eye gaps;
making way for joy,
an insistent and undeniable twin.

And when joy knocks,
we will – voices hoarse,
weakened from weeping –
strive to answer.
She, attuned to the faintest cry,
will barge in,
take charge, dry tears,
take set on[9] death and grief;
declawing the marauders,
removing the scorpions' sting.

And joy will sit with us,
sorting and saving
snatches of favourite things,
swatches of shared serendipities,
shared love, hope and – yes –
shared grief,
creating an album
of treasured, indelible memories.

We know, dear one,
such remembrances are but a bandage –
psychic plaster to hold close – for mending
the jagged edges of shattered hearts.
But they cannot contain
the largeness that is you;
an immensity of spirit
which has split the too-tight skin of earth
to fly where knowledge, music and story
are infinite.

And we will meet again, beloved,
where death and grief cannot enter;
where joy – the overcomer –
will eternally prevail,
and parting be expunged forever
from the range of human tongue,
purged from every recess of the heart.
For time and frail flesh
will have lost dominion,
never to rule again.

CHASING HYPOCRISY

Letter to the Editor of Walls and Public Billboards

Dear Sir/Madam:
I saw your note
yesterday, early,
a large billboard, corner of Fowler and Shirley,
proclaiming to the quick and spiritually dead,
"Adulterers and homosexuals
will not see God." Period.
No "ifs", hesitant subjunctives,
no mawkish conditionals,
but nicely framed in red –
simulating, as far as I could tell,
in a pithy, allusive tour de force –
the ever-burning, sulphurous fires of hell.

And – thinking we post-nuclear Thomases,
post-colonial, cell and gender revisionists,
technology theists –
would doubt;
there was that stamp of authenticity –
your signature, God, stunning in beige simplicity.
Strange… In that delicious whoredom called
Babylon,
you did not sign on the fabled wall
(your chosen writing tablet),
in Nebuchadnezzer's orgiastic banqueting hall.

But that anomaly aside…
Sir, I beg to call attention to grave omissions;
lest this new brief – though not writ in stone –
slice open to bone a society already rent
with numerous suppurating fissures.

Have you remembered no more
sins of fathers who take daughters as wife,
mothers whose ill-placed love
seduces sons to slaughter them
in effigies carved from other women's lives?
And what of betrayers of public treasury and
trust…
men who rape land, women, children;
robbing the rest of us of coin and hope,
turning souls and countries to dust?

And what of the gospel jockeys,
who sport their colours
on the silk of their tongues,
and ride religion
into the winners' circle and lordly purse
of the race-courses called church,
temple, synagogue or peristyle;[10]
there to feed from gilded collection plates
behind equally gilded altars
on crisp new currency and nubile youth;
all the while filling the troughs
of the stable hands
with land of milk and honey promises
of palaces large and exceeding fine
and places of choice and plenty
in heaven's ephemeral buffet line?

Predation

We have become ravening beasts,
perpetually engaged in frenzied feeding,
sinking our "I" teeth
into the jugular of "us",
ripping the flesh of communal life
to feed the greedy offspring of self.

Blood lust high, nostrils flaring,
we hunt down
the striped, pied, counter,[11] lame.
Slavering jaws,
greedy for newborn or ancient woes,
disembowel, devour;
letting fall choice slivers
to shrivel in the scorching sun
of public malice;
and – like hurricane ham[12]
left to hang, deformed –
sad host for defecating flies.

And satiety never comes.
The common prey exhausted
we turn to intra-species predation.

Predation II

Predators, counterfeiting sainthood,
spout blessings and gospels of freedom;
yet crouch in thickets of tainted righteousness
to ambush love,
savage neighbours' aspirations,
and suck the marrow from their dreams.

We bloodthirsty saints have no saviour.
Jesus left the building long before Elvis
died to save rock 'n roll
and make Graceland its holy place.
But Jesus is trying for a comeback;
return engagement hastened
by an urgent need to scourge …
purge the temple …
to protect the purity of his vision
from the toxic mould
invading the empty tombs of our souls.

Primacy is no longer primordial….
He'll have to up the ante,
advance the date on streets of gold.
Hollywood, eye long time
on a piece of heaven's bullish action,
is winning the bid
to restructure the gospels,
creating a creed with greater currency,
more palatable to jaded hearts.

What we need is a new god,
who will grant the miracle we truly need –
our names emblazoned
on a phallic plinth,
leaving each victor
on an otherwise barren field of triumph.

Slavery Redux

We who cut teeth on promises of paradise
frolic to the flute of a star-striped piper,
gyrating on the sword's edge
of geopolitics.

We eat, drink, sing and dance,
lulled by the illusion
of benevolence, on call
to drive us home from heedless revels,
drunk on the over-proof rum
of self-delusion.

Revels grow cold,
and soporific melodies –
pledging endless summer, sky juice,
and year-round junkanoo[13] –
will forge us new chains and manacles,
with small hope of emancipation.

Recipe

Take one or two choice dupes,
tenderize with a serpent's tongue
until they yield up their grievous stories.
Take these sad tales, and wring out
all but a teaspoon of truth.
Next, rehydrate in a stream of lies,
seasoning liberally with the spice of malice.

Now, spread your piquant mixture
over seething social networks,
whether exigent electronic media
or more leisurely backyard fence.
Watch culinary artistry
become the talk of the town;
a dish fit for the maceration of character;
a stew that sours marriages;
a ceviche to sever friendships;
an ever-flowing fount of spite,
filling the feeding troughs of thousands.

CHASING MADNESS

Rage Comes

Rage is born
where houses sag to arthritic knees
in sad, unanswered prayer;
where the future is frozen
between blowsy walls
tied up with dingy string,
and "father" is a question-mark,
or a heavy, rum-soaked hand,
or laboured rutting in an endless night.

Rage grows
when mother is a woman of Samaria,
drawing night and daily
from a deep, public well of despair;
and a child becomes a jarring note,
unwanted intermezzo
in an already flawed,
dissonant composition.

Rage ferments in dreams stillborn;
steeps in the bitter lees
of hope garotted in the womb;
and dispossession denies sunlight,
stunting love
and growth of seedlings.

Rage swells
constricted between reef and rock;
its own impotence blocking vents.
Pressure builds, magma boils,
red heat shatters rocks of resistance,
explodes the fragile cage of proscriptions.

Freed, the foul beast roars,
convulsing in pyroclastic flows
to mount and violate the living.

Rage ejaculates in violence,
its mordant seed
swelling the womb of earth with death.
And on that day the clouds don mourning,
spinning ashy cotton
into sackcloth and shrouds.

Limping to Jerusalem

The world has turned
heels over head;
its grimy feet faking passion in air,
like those of a street-corner whore
on a back-seat date;
and life is a series of gritty film-reels,
competing for depths of despair
and rating points
on rival tv stations.

If Christ were on his final stomp,
there would be no triumphal ride;
the permit for a public parade
would be late, delayed
by some uncivil, public ass;
the palms, drought-dried;
the fickle crowd soon turned aside,
seeking thrills from the opposing party.

No thorn-crowned head;
no nail-pierced hands;
no film-worthy passion at Calvary.
The legions – snide, unionized,
constantly threatening coups,
or equally bloody industrial action –
would deride weekend overtime,
taking their text from the gospel of greed.

No salvation for us;
but the cover of *Time*
for Pilate, sublime in purple,
and ascribing the non-event
to new Italian sensibilities.
Jesus would no longer be a pogrommed Jew,

but a kibbutz knight, firing child-killing volleys,
ducking dispossessed Ishmael's
self-inclusive shrapnel;
an exchange wound tight
in a looped reel of hate.

Apostles, aggrieved,
would beat a hasty retreat,
contemplating commitment
to a sonless god, readier to rout
and smite with plagues,
such as their traitor god
once rained
on recalcitrant Egypt.

Irascible Peter would seek
a redeemer for our times –
a two-fisted warlord saviour –
who, in pronouncements of tanks and thunder,
would revoke the pusillanimous gospels,
condemn as blasphemy
the turning of cheeks,
and bid Wall Street Judas
fill a war chest.

One thing would remain the same.
No matter her name, somehow, somewhere
in the aborted Nirvanas of America's alleyways,
on the arid, hungry tracks of Africa,
in the teeming, ambitious streets of Asia,
amidst the refined corruption of Europe,
or shackled to the Caribbean's
deeply discounted plantations,

a mother would be inconsolably weeping
over her broken, bloodied child.

Fearful Geometry

It often begins its infection
at the centre point of circles;
prime vantage point
for rapid dispersal.
Hate's poison gallops
in fearful geometry –
a cancer, coursing each radius,
swelling nodes, chords, segments,
silently filling the plane –
alien familiar terror,
inexorably, exponentially
expanding;
its perimeter a greedy maw,
engulfing, consuming
host community,
country, world.

Inevitability

Promised to him from birth,
she knew him, furtive lord,
but did not yet know him
in intimate intercourse.
Incestuous, catholic lover, he
claimed first her mother,
then father and brother;
leaving no one to witness
her inevitable marriage.
In fearful fascination,
she spoke often of him,
eager to lift the veil,
to map the details
of his face,
trace the lineaments
discovered daily –
in surprise,
in welcome,
or with fear-widened eyes –
by curbside car washers and car-proud czars,
pompous politicians and junglist youth,
terrorists and bible-thumpers,
milky babes and mothers,
the madding ranks of commerce,
and the harried middling sort;
all trouping in forced fealty
to his moribund kingdom.

One day…
he would claim her,
name her confidently his,
and draw the breath
from her body with his kiss.

Script Change

Blockbuster film, genre romance/adventure...

They head east on the Orient Express,
across Tigris to Baghdad,
to anise-laced days,
cinnamon-scented dreams.
Voyaging on Silk Road
to souks of mystery,
blonds from the west
with coded breasts, finger silk,
making mind flights
to eunuched harems
and khol-eyed princes;
playing ecstasy on the tambour
of Georgia-peach skin.

Sweet coffee eyes
by the thousands,
liquid enough
to set afloat a thousand and one nights.
Children with magazine-cover faces
waiting for the click
of opportunistic shutters
and chocolate bars.
Turbanned Aladdins spinning tales
on hookahed afternoons;
smoke rising
and muezzins bidding all bow
to an Allah not unwilling
to take a saucer of chai
with Christ.

Script change, genre drama/tragedy...

Baghdad blast, C4 shatters dreams.
Radical plastic surgery
reshapes landscapes, limbs and faces.
Acrid smoke, forever rising,
supplies the incense of mosques,
hallowed by priests
on jihad for Allah.
All the while cannoned tanks of Christ
and capitalism
square off against Kalashnikovs;
spitting death and new gospels
in foreign tongues,
needing no Rosetta stone
for translation.

Far from the sainted roomless inn
and the manger cradle in Bethlehem,
women with sorrow-limned eyes
– barred from the preservation register
of conscience –
carry rolled carpets
of children's bodies,
whose blood curses their assassins,
whose bullets curse back.

Award-winning photographs proliferate
for a lustful maw, greedy for broken flesh
and story-worthy despair; fresh fodder
for the evening news,
piquant side dish for consumption
with charred barbecue and fried falafel,
wrapped in yesterday's tragedy.

Now, Mohammed daily plots a journey west
to bloody the much-published face
of his more popular brother prophet.

Hawk and Dove Dialogue

Hawk
War is the perfect instrument
for building character in youth,
who waste time dreaming.
War depresses self-importance
in huddled, hungry masses,
who question our inalienable right
to rampant consumerism
and rejection of puling peace.

Dove
War is a scratching post,
where jaded jocks find ease
for the mordent itch of rabid ambition.
War is Middle East crude,
poured with profligate hand
on seething embers of despair
for speedier conflagration.

Hawk
War strips away
the shine of fairytale,
inserting the reality
of geopolitics and minefields;
suppressing insurgent tomorrows,
hobbling future militant limbs…
War satisfies the exigency
of having it our way.

Dove
War is the history book of tyrants,
battering rams in chain mail,
or metrosexual urbanites
chillingly slick in the art of Armani.

Their goose-stepping scribes
never slow to write tragedy,
pen their patrons' narratives
in the indelible ink of innocent blood –
a fount that never ceases to flow.

Hawk
War is art, story of the man's man,
the drone of its missiles, music.
War lends wings to inherent heroism,
accords a measure of satiety,
palliating the hunger for glory.
War bestows courage to cross Rubicons,
keep the bridge, cross the Alps,
face thousands with three hundred.
Hurrah and a twenty-one gun salute,
dulce et decorum est…
into the valley of death,
once more to the breach,
smart bombs and killing fields,
pro patria and chaos *mori*,
and all deliciously, bloody that.

Dove
War is the humour of the hangman,
the madman's shrill song,
screech of insanity that swallows reason,
sole choir in which fools will sing,
forever wailing the *missa solemnis*
in D for death major;
kyrie lacking *eleison*,
gloria repudiating *gloria dei*,
credo cancelling *resurrexit*.

In brief,
war anchors the climb of humanity
by a single thread;
rapidly, ineluctably unraveling.

CHASING IDENTITY

Staking Claim to Our Souls

For Neko

We are our own discoverers,
staking claim to territory
too many centuries colonized;
burning flags of conquest,
too long planted in our souls;
repurposing mind manacles,
forging keys to liberate creation.

With the hammer of pen and paintbrush
on the resilient anvil of canvas and page,
we are purging recrimination, grief, regret;
drawing from their deep dye
bold strokes of peace, metaphors of hope,
to serve as viceroy and governor
of a New World of freedom.

Fringe Dweller

I'm the fragile outer skin
of the world's tightly coiled
onion;
brown, brittle envelope
readily discarded,
guardian of succulence
that I cannot share.

I am the footnote,
separated from the main;
bottom-margined;
distanced, arcane symbol,
sought only by dogged scholars;
the dry pages that usher in
humanity's disposable chapters.

I am the dark secret
everyone knows, but few acknowledge;
Sleeping Beauty's unbidden fairy;
Owens screwing Nazi genetics;
Poitier braving the chilly dinner –
frowned upon presence
in company and conversation –
annoying fragment,
stuck between the world's teeth,
resisting persistent pick
and anti-bacterial sluice.

I am the rouser of nervous titter;
trigger for bar-room braggadocio,
justification for smug policies
of affirmative inaction,
of selective culling;
crime eliciting laws of repression,
inspiration for pseudo-science
and copious texts of repudiation.

Yet, here I am.
Here I stand.

Of Shattered Spears and Shiny Forks

Once-proud warrior,
your obsidian limbs'
strong and steady gait
once outpaced lions,
once danced you home
to praise-song of sloe-eyed girls,
strewing your path with patent desire.
Now, your hero's legs
creak in new plantation genuflection.

Now, you hunt rights
to boardroom silver,
to spear conch fritters and crab cakes.
Now, you blood your shaft
in the hearts of colleagues
less adept at betrayal.
Of your hero's howl
that once silenced Serengeti,
there's nothing left
but the flapping of your lips
in fealty to foreign gods.

Dishonoured ancestors groan,
seeking to slake Atlantic salt
that weighs down wings,
delays your flight home.
But home is no haven…
It offers you no hero's welcome,
no shriving from the gods,
who scorn your false libations.

You cannot pass to natal ground
by cloaking your sins in kente cloth.
Sika futuro[14] cannot transmute
base metal into gold.
Elegba[15] has rolled up the roads
engineering confusion.
Drunk on palm wine
Obatala cannot dispense clarity.
And Bumba now vomits merlot,
merchandizing diamonds, rape and death.
Eshu's once hallowed breath
now stinks of caviar from a Black Sea
more beautifully black than his errant soul.
Like you, the gods now barter brethren
for false smiles, false friends,
and jaguars with a diesel roar.

Brother man, you have been weighed
and your measure falls short.
Sacrifice of cellophaned lamb
cannot absolve you;
flames of impassioned rhetoric
will not reburnish your spear.
Your blade must be tempered anew
in sacred fires of contrition
and the ice-cold stream
of truth.

I want to go Caribbean

I want to go Caribbean,
to the Haiti that is
not Labadee.[16] Don't want to go
where sovereign of the sea
and white whale beach
sheltered from surf
where black bodies float
bloated with drink
from ocean's hospitality.

I want to go Caribbean,
rove Leeward, row Windward,
reject Ritz and three-star culture,
forego the night tour
on Colombian mule,
and find the spot in Guyana forest
where the six peoples meet as one.

I want to drink up Barbados
beyond the pubs,
see T & T[17] behind the mask,
and explore a Cuba whose deep chest
still proudly heaves beneath the heft
of our fat neighbour's boonggy.[18]

I want to go Caribbean but it far, $600 far;
Miami sniffer dog and immigration far;
CARICOM conundrum far;
free movement of people far.[19]

And sometimes…
sometimes when I reach,
is door lock, blind screw tight,
and neighbour youth bawlin'
"Go home, Hag,
'fore we strip off your J C Penney[20] skin
and salt it down."

Should be, "Long time, gal we never see you;
come mek we hol' your hand."
I want to lament your lamentations,
commend and condemn you,
godmother your children,
marry my daughters to your sons,
validate the "us" in shared plantations,
draw life from bartered bloodlines.

But, until then…
Let's share peas 'n rice and aspirations
Cuba bound and Cuba Libres
mofongo,[21] Jamaica jerk[22]
and Bahamian guava duff.[23]
Let's celebrate Junkanoo, Cropover, Carnival,[24]
wine down[25] to pan[26] and goombay drum,[27]
share the common and the grand,
dance to dancehall and the downfall
of cowboy diplomacy,[28]
and soon-come, new-colonial woes.

Come Brother, Sister, Cousin Caribbean!
Come make me see myself in your eyes!
Come see yourself in mine!

Remembering, Re-membering

My name was scraped from the register
of the griot's tongue
and fed to sharks, whose memory is short
except for blood;
and long ago, my captive member
was wrenched from the sweetness of yours.

Remember me?
I'm the pricking of memory in your loins.
Press your ear against my breast,
hear your drums pulsing still in my blood,
let their throbbing send your heart racing
past coffle and castle,
beyond forced couplings in foreign lands.
Strip away the long cloak of separation,
rend my bodice of bondage,
shred the rough girdle of shame.

Grip me once again
in your baobab arms,
bind me with the lianas of your heart,
bathe me in your potent Congo,
cradle my head again
in the thick savannas
of your seething breast…

Call me yours again!
Re-member me,
grow me a griot's tongue to tell ancestral tales,
give me warrior's legs to leap the rough Atlantic
chasm
and arms to embrace the freedom that is mine by
right.

Let me – with heart and hands wide open –
grasp your immensity,
let my roots plunge into your soul's soil,
knitting an indissoluble re-union.

Baptism

No sooner had the child emerged,
she picked him up,
still covered in primal slime,
and she, weak from her labours,
fled the room,
engaging fleet time in a race
to show her child his birthright;
which, beguiled by the charm
of an imported Jacob's tongue,
his grandfather Esau –
sans payment in pottage –
had blindly surrendered.

Her journey seemed unending;
as if
she had entered the corridors of perspective
in a work of classical art,
where possibilities are static,
dynamic potential locked forever
in the fleshless fingers of a long dead artist;
as if
the patch of blue she pursued
were the elusive, ever more distant
vanishing point.

Trudging hour after weary hour,
she came at last to gates
wired, cctv'd, manned;
its crisp steel finials
transmuted to menacing crest
of a crouching, ancient beast;
every awesome, daunting aspect
amplified by the mystery of night.

As midnight became memory,
the guardians of the looming monster
relinquished vigilance, long relaxed
by years of non-occurrence.
Gently, she pushed her precious bundle
through the rails, then climbed –
timing her movements to the rising and sinking
of heads, fighting the superior claims of sleep.

She paused for a moment…
unbelieving,
astonished that she had breached
barriers established before her birth,
perhaps before time,
at the moment of creation.
She quickened unsteady steps,
nostrils flaring,
adjusting their receptors
to the tang of salt air,
bay geranium,
spider lilies;
sharing the instinct of feral animals,
attuning to the rank odours
of recently ruptured
amniotic sacs.

Rousing dull strength, she ran
past porticos of Carrara marble,
pavements of Mexican tile;
past deep, satisfied slumbers
over precisely engineered lawns'
crisp, exotic grass;

persuaded to abandon objections
to foreign soil
by expensive chemicals,
cow dung,
and an army of underpaid
exotic gardeners.

At last, she stopped,
transfixed by the crushed nacre glow
of the broad expanse
separating the sleeping land
from the sacred waters.
When first she felt the cold, wet sand
in the spaces between her toes,
she trembled and began to remember
what she wished her son
to know and remember.

She immersed her body,
drawing the child with her
into water that still held
sun in its silken embrace
and memories screened
in rapid, unceasing succession –
spirit memories of brown Lucayans,
fleeing dread Caribs
in the same swift canoes
that later welcomed Spaniards,
who thought hawks' bells,
red beads and smiling lies
payment enough
to annul the souls of their hosts.

Tribal memories of pale Englishmen
poured forth;
white men spurned like slaves
by their brethren
for contrary creed and doctrine,
learning the lore of the sea
to come to terms, bond
with a raw new land.

Womb memories of Yoruba
Bacongo, Ibo, Woloff, Fulani –
brotherhood fused
in the filth of death ships,
befouling the breast
of an unwilling Atlantic;
terror of the unknown,
covert resolution to defy
death and bondage,
to live as new, self-coined creations.

She recalled lived memories
of maritime joy
flooding in with the tide;
young strong limbs
cleaning goat entrails
in the flushing ebb,
beating clothes on sun-baked rocks;
head rush of ozone,
scrubbing thought barnacles
from tired city brains;
children laughing in the Easter surf,
adventuring on inner tubes,
rambling for sweet-tart seagrapes,[29]
cottony cocoplums,[30]
astringent almonds and acid tamarinds,

sampling fresh conch dipped in the brine,
gin and coconut water jollity,
savour of hot macaroni and cheese,
hickory bite of barbecue,
goat-peppered potato salad,
hotdogs propelled
by slippery mayonnaise and too tight grip
out of bread jacket into inedible sand;
surprised young faces swelling,
tears welling,
regatta sails bellying in wind,
aging asthmatic mail boats,
wheezing from port to port;
swift jab of urchin spines,
surreptitious release of bladder,
acid sting of jellyfish,
salt tang tingling tongue,
nostrils burning,
eyes opening to briny treasures,
whorled mystery of the brain,
breezy art of the fan,
fear of the scalding fire,
wonder of tiny fish –
swimming in faultless formation
obeying primordial programmes –
serendipity of a playful pod
of dolphins breaching the waves,
passing orcas creating shifting islands,
she crabs flushing eggs
in the progeny cycle,
millions of their children rising
like rushing red tides –
sprightly thousands
to be mangled dry
on trafficked roads,
bracelets of fishy seaweed
clinging to brown limbs –

lovers entwined, oblivious
of any life but theirs;
heroic dreams sculpted in sand,
wind and wave bearing tales
of other lands,
net floats of pastel glass,
pride of Portuguese fishing fleets,
sundown tales of rum-cured salts,
salt rime on drying skins…

Overcome, brain exploding,
she yelled the same yell
of birthing,
feeling the same wrenching pain
of irreversible separation.
In fevered, frantic motion,
she dipped her baby
again and again
in the never still, never silent tide;
inviting it to whisper in his ear,
imprint on his skin
a lifetime of salt memories
to savour;
to treasure like wrecked galleon gold,
lightening his life sentence
of sea-less days.

CHASING FREEDOM

Conversation with God

It's not easy
to broach a conversation with God,
with your compass determinedly askew,
and you, struggling to steer clear
of the shoals and reefs
crowding your life.

It's not easy;
pot boiling over,
antediluvian dog barking at ghosts
– scared up by canine dementia –
squalling child on one arm;
husband finding solace
in the arms of commerce
and a tight-bodied bimbo.
It's not easy to engage a being
who calls himself
an uncompromising
often incomprehensible
all-encompassing I Am.

But, one fine day,
my courage stoked
to a shaky boil,
making every effort to squelch the squalls,
dismiss the demented dog,
dispatch spouse, business and bimbo
to the ash heap of inconsequential memory,
I began, "Lord, free me."

He answered
in that stingy, clipped fashion
He has used with success
from Genesis to Revelations
to discourage questions
requiring revealing
pre-apocalyptic replies,
"Free yourself."

Then, relenting,
He said in his best Bahamian,
"Darlin''', wha' you want?
I gie you free will!
Is you choose to entertain duh cheat,
birth duh child and feed duh dog.
But, daughter, my phone number in the book.
I'n no civil servant yuh know,[31]
I does answer all calls
with no political beef,
an' my grace enuf fuh you."

Gaulin Women[33]

I will no more weep bitter tears
for women who cradle sons
whose bodies, seasoned
with leaden peppercorns,
are dressed for the feast
of a voracious grave.

Nor mourn for women whose lonely breasts
ache for sucklings who never were,
for babes whose tender bodies
lie in the raw, gaping graves
of withered wombs
of dreams too long deferred.

I will no longer wail for women
whose flesh burns to dance
where society's piper calls no tune;
whose passions must skulk unseen
to snatch at illicit fruit,
or cool in shaded pools of covert dreams.

I will screw tight the tap of my sorrow
for women whose secret chest of hopes
and carefully guarded sorrows
cherish costly unmentionables: –
wan silk never stroked in passion,
rice and rose petals never strewn,
white satin and ribbons now yellowed and sere,
lacy veils never lifted for the kiss,
that brings promise into joyful presence.

Instead, you gaulin women
left to hunger by hypocrisy,
exiled from the congregation
of your exemplary sisters,
paraded naked down streets
of two-faced, snide contempt;
I bid you distill to potent alchemy
anger, desire and despair,
to split the skin that binds your wings.

Then rise, rise, rise to new horizons…

Rise up from blows
of your own self loathing,
rise up from barren longing.
Rise up together;
and with a mighty beating of wings
open long-bound throats
in strident chorus,
trumpeting in brazen notes
your right to weep,
your right to shout,
your right to love,
your right to sing.

A Witch's Tale

From the eighth day in Eden,
the serpent – standing accused,
still scintillating in rainbow scales,
and determined to diffuse condemnation –
pointed to First Woman, hissing,
"Strega!"[34]

Though his tongue
split on the sharp edge of the lie,
he – still linguistically agile,
tongue twisting the truth –
branded Woman's daughters,
soucouyant,[35]
obeah woman,
worker of iniquity,
witch;
issuer of foul blood,
pouring from the fissure
cleft for Woman's sin,
poisoning the earth.

He called us beasts,
creatures of unseemly pendants,
soft secret places
that turn heads athwart,
set loins burning,
bending minds and bodies
to our scabrous will.

In the forge of this first fabrication,
malice fashioned nightmares:
fuel to feed the shrieks of hysterics,
recasting the vulnerable
as riders of wind and satan's warty member,
blighters of corn, cattle and innocence,
spoilers of the fruit of the womb,
authors of unholy screams in mists of dawn,
mistresses of foul things that creep at night,
dancing naked and widdershins to gibbous moons,
feasting on the flesh of unweaned babes,
nourishing desires defiling creation.

Since then Eve's daughters have stood
accused, condemned,
inquisitioned over steam iron and hot fat
for the heresy of woman's right
to freedom.

We are
held in contempt in courting power,
imprisoned by the weight of old wives tales,
life-sentenced to do hard time,
crushed beneath glass ceilings,
hanged from the gibbet of lies,
necks near broken
by the noose of womanhood.

Caribbean Sweetheart

Caribbean woman,
mighty silk cotton tree;
buttressing nascent nations,
roots spanning triangle
of Atlantic water,
how now you can turn
sugarcane for sugar daddy
to suck dry
and toss your husk to pigs?

Mother of Jah,[36]
of the sistren of Nanny,[37]
Seacole,[38] Dames Doris[39] and Eugenia[40] –
strong, righteous women –
how now can you feign love for gain,
plunging
from the contested heights
of self-aware womanhood
onto the scorching desert breast
of male lust?

If they could,
Godiva of the horse,
Joan of Arc,
Nanny of the Maroons,
Seacole of the lamp,
Amanda of the bloomers;[41]
Sojourner of the truth,[42]
Rosa of the bus[43]
would descend
from woman's heaven,
taking up arms for a new crusade
to rescue you from the cane patch.

Poetic Licence

I cavil at constraints imposed by modern critics,
who bid poets abandon the freedom
of ancient convention.
They sneer at synecdoche,
forbid figures,
outlaw onomatopoeia;
leading the unwary
into the follies and snares,
deceits and conceits,
of free verse.

I declare my independence!

On rutting afternoons of rain,
with the aid of grinning, gap-toothed caesura,
I breach the dank wall of doctoral disapproval.
In its cold, imposing shadow,
I play with pliant plosives, float
adrift on fluid alexandrines,
shag an ever-willing Shakespeare –
that bawdy English bard,
who put sex into sextets
and hid concupiscence in quatrains

Sweeping aside the oil slick of prohibition,
I plunge into the lovely liquids
of sensual alliteration.

And some days –
some beautiful languid days –
my foot slips altogether
from the tightrope of righteousness;
plunging past Propriety,
sitting tight-lipped and prim
on its lonely promontory.
I fall, arms flailing, skirt flying overhead,
revealing fat, sensuous rhythm and rhyme.

As the day wanes and the moon waxes,
I lie replete in the arms of my sister,
the imp of improvisation;
remembering nothing,
revisioning nothing,
interrogating nothing,
contesting nothing.

Solace

One day,
amidst chic chatter,
purposeful petitions,
the painful carving of rungs
for the climb oft denied;
impotent pleas
to deaf gods of government,
and packaged, sanctioned greed,
the sun, so sure,
so slowly,
will begin its decline
in a moment unmarked by history,
unsung by us,
the women of unmotherly ambition.

Then…
Then…
The towering, clashing chords
of ambitious life –
the yin, the yang;
the heat, sturm und drang –
will segue smoothly
into piano passages
seldom breached by crescendo,
where we're forced to embrace
the false dignity of whispers,
sipping bittersweet tea
and sympathy.

Then…
Then…
in a moment of hiatus –
in a break from the humming
of busy, charitable,
matronly bees –
in a pause from desultory boasts
of purposeful yesterdays
and prodigious feats
of ambitious progeny,
I'll look out
and spy with gladness
the bird that snobs the V
of instinctive convention;
diverging,
not blindly following,
brave outrider of the norm.

I'll mark the fall
of a lonely leaf
and my heart will leap
to see it dancing,
defying the stillness
of the windless day,
resisting;
mocking
the imminence
of decay.

Then…
Then…
I'll laugh,
dance,
sing
in fellow feeling,
sweetening dry destiny
with the mead
of wry life,
thumbing my nose,
flashing the finger
in time's ever mobile face.

On The Effects of a Note Played by Wynton Marsalis

Wynton – trapped,
languishing in electronic limbo
in the guts
of Ms Rose's
new state-of-the-art
Bose[44] sound system –
mined a silver note
from the motherlode
of sweet, jook[45] dance;
children borning,
Junkanoo New Year's morning:
some call it slack;
moonless midnight black music.

The note –
high-born, sassy,
lording it in the ranks
of tonal revolution,
somewhere above
high C –
screamed its freedom,
hovering for a moment
over Miss Rose's
dozing,
blue-haired friends.

Then, that clean, bold sharp
skated down the scale,
still sweet enough
to pierce the soul,
and, swift as a kick
from her Harry's customary brew,

collided with a soulmate
deep in Miss Rose's
repressed, somnolent heart;
a place Harry had never touched
in forty years
of shared bills,
shared children,
and now shared blood-pressure pills,
because he didn't even –
couldn't even – know,
because Rose herself didn't know,
it was there.

For a moment –
just for a moment –
she sat,
panicked,
clinging
to the outcropping
of unyielding rock
that was her life;
a stony face,
barren, silent,
except for stubby growths
of myrrh
and the cackle
of predatory Bingo crows;
a plateau
that adamantly refused
to sprout peaks of ecstasy.

Sitting tight
In the narrow confines
of her skinny, dry tower,
wrapped for warmth
in her thick coat of dusty doctrine,
and a patrimony of prejudice,

Miss Rose felt
the heavy moist note
seep through unguarded cracks,
and trembled
when it burst into
quivering semiquavers
of startling arpeggios.

One more blast of the trumpet,
and Rose's Jericho
lay bare,
open to ravishing
by passion's virile Joshua.

Then
that monumental emotion –
camouflaged so well
by electronic wizardry –
heated her innards
to incandescence,
melting her
stainless-steel will,
loosening the whalebone corset
of adamant denial
that stifled her heart;
admitting that gigolo of a note.

Miss Rose yelped
like a scalded lap dog
unused to injury.

She thus spoke her first word
in the language of passion,
unuttered in forty years
of marriage to a man
sparing of words
in any tongue.

This couldn't be;
she, Rose, was a woman
... of dignity.

She felt her vital juices
flow from the centre of her gut,
hot and sweet –
like her orange-tinged barbecue sauce –
to tingle every extremity.
"Resurrection..." she gasped;
her breath snagged
in the invisible net of sound,
swinging between
woofers and tweeters.
"This is what the Great Getting-up
Morning is gonna feel like."

Galvanized
by the volcanic mudslide
down the monolith
of her soul,
Miss Rose –
to her absolute horror –
rose from her chair,
and right in front
of all her blue-haired friends,
she let that hungry silver note
sweet talk her pelvis.

From some unidentified
hotspot in that concavity,
rose a wave of rapture;
riding her neural pathways
until her whole body
pulsed in the giant
slow, rhythmic S's
of a suspension bridge,

whose point of harmonic resonance
has been attained.

The torrid *pas seul* ended
when Miss Rose's
long, slow shudder
jerked to a stop
with a jolting thrust of her hips
in a bump and grind
Josephine Baker
would have died
to call her own.

A blue-haired eye
popped open:
Sweet Jesus,
Rose having the spirit
Or doing a obeah dance!
The single eye
– startled –
remained ajar,
stuck fast
by the glue of surprise.

Just for a moment –
No, just for the interstice
between seconds –
Miss Rosie, gospel-hall gracious,
ever careful of character,
her rhythms long ago adjusted
to march tunelessly
in time to the lugubrious fugue
of her father's values,
the two-finger 'Chopsticks'
of Harry's aspirations,
the querulous stingy staccato
of a critical community,

had vibrated like a tuning fork.
Her resonance to that note –
a deep, foundation-rattling rising –
would have been unbearable
if sustained by that ill-used
instrument.

But, though brief,
the reverberation
of inner space
was wild enough,
free enough
to share chords with the universe
and show Miss Rose
what it was
just to be.

Woman Unconquerable

I am woman,
reputed rib from Adam's side,
assigned voiceless subordination,
relegated to the role of sidekick,
servant to penile supremacy,
daily peeling the mazorca,[47]
jaw frozen in rictus,
knees locked in genuflection
of unnegotiated servitude.

Yet, here I am,
refusing reduction,
head unbowed, tongue unchained;
resisting devaluation
of self-forged new coinage.

I'm "Third World" woman,
mistress of the alchemy of hunger,
daily spinning life from straw of scarcity.
Is ancient Japanese kaprang[48] I ride,
we two daily mounting insurrection,
braving pothole, detour and downpour,
fighting fickleness of two-faced economy;
all on shame-brand, threadbare tires,
her joints creaking a duet with mine
in ready-to-retire sisterhood.

I am a witch of Gambaga,[49]
by the twin spells
of custom and spite,
transmuted
from wife, wise woman, mother,
into poisoner of mates, minds and wombs;

Satan's doxy, covert holder
of his proxy for evil,
my fate steered by the compass
of a dying fowl's wings.

Yet, scrawny yard-bird that I've become,
I scratch up sustenance from the dust,
conjure up purpose, and cling –
rotten tooth and bony claw –
to life.

I am every woman.
I pay passage but never reach
the market called "freedom";
my fruit spoiling in fetid cage
and claustrophobic crate,
shut in and shut out
by tariff, quota,
disease and domination,
ignorance and interdiction,
my flight to higher heights
often hijacked, shot down.

But still, I am, I live;
a woman, mistress
of unconquerable convictions.

Now, meet this sister,
steel forged in magma-spilling mountains
tempered in chill Tongue of Ocean depth,
bold Atlantic/Caribbean woman,
hands akimbo,
liberal and bent on liberation,
broad of beam, deep of voice,
brave and feisty for days,

raucously refusing
to travel bound again,
below deck again.

Go ahead, Lords of Fraud
and tainted tenure,
repossess the kaprang,
foreclose the shack,
cancel my right to community,
refuse note and certification,
cancel permit and visa,
invoke self-interested sanction,
trample on my aspirations,
slam your door in my face.

Like loa-duppy-jumbie-sperrit,[50]
I'll haunt your dreams.

Dis me nah! Caribbean Buttercup,
colonizer of roadside ditch,
conqueror of desolate ground,
queen gilding a glorious kingdom
from a stinking, ancient rubbish heap.

I ain't goin' nowhere;
this land and me is one.
Deny me rain and I run wild;
prune me and I'll coppice;
rip off my blooms and I'll reseed;
root me up and I'll spring back
to flourish in your face.

They're Dancing

They're dancing
to the beat of a band in Egypt,
tuning rusty instruments
to play nearly forgotten notes
of unfettered expression.

They're dancing with halting steps
to long-forgotten tones
of ten movement music,
struggling to revive the glories
of Pear Garden Academy,[51]
celebrating a budding renaissance
of graceful dance.

All over the world,
Unheralded,
unexpected notes
have set metronomes ticking,
tuning forks humming,
composers venturing
into less common chords.

Some, soon discouraged,
will abandon their scores
to be feted only in festoons of cobwebs
and rheumy-eyed recounting
of glories almost grasped.

Some, envisioning power and pedestals,
will recruit the harshest notes
to beat out the brass and blare
of strident martial music.

A rare few
– weary from a midnight's labour –
will catch sight of the sun,
orchestrating morning,
linking light to life
in a faultless score.
Seduced by the grace of nature's accords,
these few, scattered, seldom-sung
makers of truest music
will strive for uncommon harmonies,
exalting consonance and peace.

But we performers must call the tunes
to which we will dance,
choose bands suited to our instruments,
conductors inspired to interpret our notes,
drum-majors worthy of unquestioned following;
before we commit
to mount the stage,
to join the parade,
to dance.

CHASING LIGHT

Beauty Is Not Partial

True beauty is not partial,
does not discriminate,
does not care
with whom she lies
to share the joy
of her bounty.

Generous, often profligate,
she spreads herself equally
in manger and mansion,
over untamed field
and formal garden,
gracing rustic board no less
than lordly table.

In equal portion beauty pairs
Winter's august austerity
with the pied playfulness of Spring,
cacophony of crow
with the lyrebird's velvet plaint.
She crowns with blessing downy youth,
yet confers upon the furrowed face
her profoundest benediction.

Beauty is mystery.
Her richest enchantment often lies
where purblind, jaundiced eyes
see only impairment,
and bigotry daily, foolishly mocks
beauty's most munificent bounty.

Pittsburgh Spring

Nature plotted a grand exhibition
of her daughter's sensuous proclivities;
letting fall broad hints
of her darling's flirtations,
her skill at luring birds,
bronzed from long tropic vacations,
her irresistible allure
when flashing her freesias,
dazzling with her dahlias,
letting slip glimpses of ranunculus red;
all in a slow seduction
to rouse sleeping earth.

Then, lordly, blustering Winter –
Nature's cold and angry son –
flung down proscription
in thick blankets of white,
aborting sunshine and premature blooming,
censoring his sister's rash frivolity.

But, as he knew she would,
knew she could,
Nature sloughed off the frigid coat,
laid bare her daughter's
impeccable charms,
turning on her passionate ally, the sun,
in a show of irrepressible power.

Light Music

Five light, feathered notes –
divine semiquavers –
sat upon a steel and aluminum stave
sketching a late-winter chord
in a minor key.
For a moment,
the grand movement stilled,
muting the brassy clash of conflict,
lightening the basso profundo
of the soul's customary plaints.
Then silence staged the soaring
of five brief notes –
an incipient sonata, taking wing –
a presto in a sunless sky.

Chasing Blues

In the chill of northeast Trades,
slipping past Gulf Stream's tropic grip,
ruching blue satin sea with lace of foam;
I chase blues with coffeehouse rock,
mind running riffs with Nickel Creek,
up and down the hills of "Smoothie Song".

I'm suffused with glow of caffeine;
heart boogying
under porcelain blue sky morning,
keeping the beat of waking bird-song.

'Prisoned only by bars of sunlight;
my spirit floats free, pirouettes in air,
soaring above deep navy blue,
where whales rule,
and haunting whalesong
hits the top of ocean charts.

Blithe spirit, she swoops
where blue-green Taino stepping-stones
tryst with powder-white calcareous sand,
kissing in an aquamarine crystal dream
where proud scions of Africa –
centuries and a long-slaked sorrow from home –
cling; scraping recalcitrant life from fragile lime,
resigned that return passage is figment,
scant memory, dim dream, attenuated filament;
losing the struggle for survival
amid the stridency and tangle
of New World certainties and bloodlines.

Blues bring welcome surfeit,
Sugared treats for an already full soul.
And I eat and drink in children's party greed,
sky, sea, island, birds, home;
multicoloured people song, kaleidoscopic story,
stuffing senses with a feast of sweetmeats
'til mind and heart, grown fat on delight,
crack the cocoon of daily doubts
to free a butterfly of inexpressible joy.

These Few Words

For Neko

You and I run fast,
have run so long together,
steps in tandem,
milestones synchronized;
we begin to think
we are but one pair of legs,
one pair of lungs,
one heart;
but time the unraveler
seems fleeter,
committed to separation.

So, while she remains
a scant length behind,
I give you these few
words; inadequate,
but all I have to convey the height,
depth and breadth of what you are,
will ever be to me.
I would live every second, hour, day,
again; make of our shared race
a recording sealed forever on repeat.

But then, why should we fear time,
or flagging steps?
True love, fed by love divine,
is not subject to errant breeze,
compass deviation,
change of clock or clime;
but outruns the tyranny of years
and cruel tongues;
short circuits grave and gravity…
dies not.

What matters slight philosophy,
when we're not dull, sublunary lovers,
junctioned by evanescent sense alone;
when your sun makes my morning rise,
and my moon silvers your night;
when love has burnt your substance
deep intaglio in my soul?

Wherever my essence shall fly
hereafter, there you will be;
and we'll run again unbound,
joyously two,
yet indissolubly one.

Today…

Yesterday, like a nyctinastic leaf,
I curled, stricken, soul pretzeled;
fearing tyranny of men and fissured earth,
crying out against a nuclear age gone nova,
mourning DNA knotting in nets of madness;
frozen by a world melting down in horror
of holocaust and impending night.

But not today…

Today, I'll unfold like morning,
lifting my face to sunlight
like waking mimosa and tamarind leaves.
I'll chase beauty, hunting in her countless haunts,
scent the must of her perfume in petrichor,
spy her green fire in the emerald flash
of a humming-bird's jeweled breast,
capture her prism in a rain-blanched sky,
toast her spirit in the burgundy of sunset.

Today, I'll pursue wild music,
pulse to the djembe[52] of my lover's heart,
dance a clamorous flamenco staccato,
syncing with rain's syncopation on rooftop
bongos.
I'll snatch song from the wail of wind,
catch it sounding in retreat of surf;
sweet rough susurrus of riotous ocean,
tonguing and silvering sun-warmed sand.

Today, I seek serenity,
ensconced in the fecund sorrow
of Walcott's sonnet sequence;
Caribbean splendour of sin and song,
humankind redeemed and rising in majesty.
Today, I claim sanctuary,
where rose windows frame the blue of heaven
and saints are living, sentient beings,
channeling in filigreed communion
the salving divinity of inner peace.

Spring Cleaning

Someday, fee in mouth, I'll cross the Styx,
ferried by the saturnine, sordid god.
Or, rewarded by a sweeter theology,
mount on wings to streets of gold…
But no descending or mounting
today.

Today, I'll clean house;
scrub windows
long grimed with gloom,
sweep away cobwebs
of ponderous care,
air closets choked with secrets
and dread of condemnation.

Spring cleaning done,
I'll throw open doors,
And welcome the flood of life.
Just once, I will
plunge naked into its turbid stream,
chase joy, fleet-foot
through corridors of freedom,
luxuriate in the lightness of being,
open soul shutters,
surf the wind,
slide laughing
down sunbeams of morning.

Poems are…

Poems are thoughts,
feelings, impulses, coalescing
points of unfettered light,
kaleidoscopic swirls
of colours, textures, tastes, sounds,
seething fluxes, words inchoate
seeking definition;
careening round corners of the mind,
through its serpentine corridors,
past dead ends, detours and diversions;
sifting through the debris of experience,
rummaging, rifling, ransacking
mountainous stores of meaning;
recalculating trajectories;
rejecting false leads,
mad flight, febrile delirium
to find the key to free the spirit
from its suffocating restraints,
from the cold iron cage
of life.

Words

Nine thousand, nine hundred ninety-nine…
not enough to sketch a life,
a philosophy, a perspective.
Must make ten thousand,
or ever more imposing
numbers of words, round, orotund,
fraught with meaning, fragrant.
Words orgasmic, prismatic,
clear Atacama dry,
foggy cloud forest wet,
coconut husk rough,
green corn silk soft,
words unguent not unctuous,
words incisive, inviting, inclusive….
Small feat,
when words in my lexicon
of life and joy
are numberless, numinous.

Words prime…
home – jigsaw puzzle of water and wonder
husband – maddening multi-sided magnificent
son – gentle giant genius
sisters, brothers, friends –
security blanket enfolding
holding love.

Words collective…
archipelago, family, community, nation,
region, hemisphere, world,
constellation, galaxy, cosmos.

Words midsummer-sea warm…
personhood, womanhood,
brother and sisterhood,
hearth and heart,
harmony and healing.

Words memorial…
of mother and father,
of obstacles overcome,
of rungs reached and passed,
of civilizations that rose,
of civilizations razed.

Words plaiting strands of sanity…
possibility, potential, pardon,
promise of everlasting peace.

Words of sound…
Wind winding, keening
round corners of September,
gurgle of gentle backwater purling,
eruption of spume through rifts in rock;
Hens clucking in corn-scattered
backyard comfort;
Nina singing smokily
of sugar in her bowl;
Mozart mining sweetness
from the strings of violins.

Words of light…
Firefly incandescence,
Bioluminescence,
refulgence of new-day glory,
peacock prismatic iridescence,
greenflash of Bahama parrot,
refraction of raindrops,
radiating rainbows,

roseate flight
of foraging flamingos,
lightning swoop of hunting raptor,
flame of sunset
rouging the grey cheeks of the ocean,
dressing for a star-studded evening.

Words of taste and texture…
Green tamarind tongue-tying,
bitter-sweet aftertaste
of soured friendship,
orange voluptuousness
of overripe mango,
sweet salt lick of lover's skin.

Words of perfume…
heady chill of hydrocarboned underground,
life-filled musk of mangroved pond,
ozone high of churning ocean,
gardens greening and gardenia'd,
sad fields solaced by star of jasmine,
powdery bouquet of new-washed baby,
smoky redolence of votive candles
and incense wafted from a swinging censer.
Christmas new painted, spruce-spiced;
orange-peeled, gingered,
cloved and cinnamoned;
kiss of sapodilla ambrosia'd lips.

Words materializing thought and wish…
Freedom freed from guns and bias,
drug lords purgatoried
in fields of burning coca,
murder murdered,
rape repudiated,
child abusers judged
by juries of children,

multinationals made stateless,
greedy financiers forced to gorge
on dry platefuls of greenbacks,
warmongers exiled to worlds
where intelligent life is
impervious to war.

Words of hope...
Jesus, greater than imprecation
or glue and fringe of junkanoo,
promise of heaven,
sweeter than Swiss chocolate,
life itself – verdant, gem-filled Eldorado,
field for endless exploration,
redundant, recurrent…
eternal.

Chasing Light collects Patricia Glinton-Meicholas's best, most powerful and urgent poems to date.

Patricia Glinton-Meicholas formalizes society's casual disregard so it is framed, gilded even, in the halls of municipality where a reader's encounter with it will make all the difference. Progress is built on paintings and poems made to summon emotional clarity at times when we have all but destroyed recognition of the fact that we are human, and sentient.

Her language is crisp – delightfully and unexpectedly because Patricia Glinton-Meicholas' subjects are also often the victims and assumptions of preoccupied people and typically denied a triumphant line in any language. She reveals anonymous others and grave observations, as the tired but vigilant seer in humanity's hands.

Here is the inked blood of an essential 21st Century writer, whose Caribbean might as well be the globe (her poem 'Baptism' should be a call to action, a wrenching candid anthem for a cautionary tale). In the world of what's deemed to be "important news", Glinton-Meicholas, the unafraid shepherd, leads us to consider those less fortunate who are barely concisely included as society trades their deprived needs for business.

Authority, speech-writer, national-freelance-curator of the arts, there can be no hypocrisy: as poet she writes from the most humane place, showing *mercy* where too little is shown outside the refuge of poetry's pain-bent eyes and humanitarian relief. Glinton-Meicholas mothers her refugee subjects in the most attentive and personal ways. She would have made a good Sister of Charity (but for her tongue, sharp as the barbs that prick politics and unchecked complacent postures she bravely calls out to task). *Chasing Light* offers literal breathing and open windows to what we'd rather not witness; her poems are "social studies" at a time when our various communities across the earth are too willing to overlook others in deep and tragic need. They are also gorgeously rendered from a solid voice that loves the timbre a human voice can make.

So, now: do we take to television "to lend credence" or do we sit and rise again with Glinton-Meicholas's poems – and *then* watch, with conscientious scrutiny, until we become witness and shepherd ourselves into the future with informed language, broad melody, and even the most subtle and overlooked rhythms? "And when joy knocks / we will – voices hoarse, / weakened from weeping – / strive to answer." Then, then – some freedom and light for our path. Thanks to Patricia Glinton-Meicholas, may it be so. May this be all the rage.

Peter Money
Vermont, U.S.A.
September 2013

We are our own discoverers

The poetry of Patricia Glinton-Meicholas is suffused with a love for language in all its myriad forms. "Coconut-husk women" – both Bahamian and archetypal – populate her writing, and she is concerned both with the personal and the political, but these are parables accessible to all, and the poetic journey she offers her readers is cyclical: a movement of pursuit where journey, not endpoint is key. Set out in five movements, the poet first looks to the light: urging us to "rise up to new horizons"; to avoid the kinds of reprehensible people who prove "grim shadows at our doors". She turns her keen poetic gaze overtly onto these shadows in the second section, 'Chasing Hypocrisy', moving thematically through Madness, Identity, Freedom and finally looping back to the precious glimpses with which she began: "Light will come again / demanding entrance."

Her writing is both scholarly and inclusive, and she reflects on her own creative process as a fall, flailing, floating into the poems she discovers: "skirt flying overhead". This collection is the tale of a true adventurer: inviting the reader to take her hand and join her as she ventures into the unknown, for, as she acknowledges so joyfully in one of the poems dedicated to her husband Neko, "We are our own discoverers."

Viki Holmes
Discovery Bay
Hong Kong
October 2013

Notes

[1] Ayiti: Haitian Creole for "Haiti"; comes directly from the language of the Taino people, Haiti's first recorded inhabitants.

[2] Derived from West African traditions, Mami Wata (water mother) is a mermaid goddess of the Haitian Vodou religion.

[3] Creole for "Our Father who art in heaven" or the French, "Notre Père qui est au ciel".

[4] La Sirène: a female member of the Haitian Vodou pantheon. She is queen of the seas, most often represented as a beautiful mermaid.

[5] L'Artibonite: Haiti's longest and most important river.

[6] Loa: see note 50 below.

[7] Coyaba: the concept of heaven believed in by the Taino people of the Caribbean.

[8] Yemaya, Our Lady of Waters, Nana, are all meant to represent Yemanja/Yemoja, an orisha or manifestation of God in the religious belief system of the Yoruba people of West Africa and known as a fierce protector of children. This deity came to the Americas with enslaved Africans and became "La Sirène" in Haiti.

[9] Take set on: Bahamian expression for "direct fixed attention to", "attack".

[10] Focal point of worship in the Haitian Vodou rites.

[11] Counter: used to signify "contrary", "adverse", "going against the norm", etc.

[12] Hurricane ham: Conch (*strombus gigas*) air-dried for preservation; a major food source for Bahamians before refrigeration was available.

[13] Junkanoo: is the masquerade tradition of The Bahamas, staged most spectacularly in the early hours of Boxing Day and New Year's Day, but also used on a smaller scale to enliven other special occasions.

[14] *Sika futuro* (or "gold dust") is a kente textile woven for the use of royals.

[15] Elegba, Obatala, Bumba (or Mbombo) and Eshu are African Deities. Mbombo is the lord of creation who vomited up all that lives on the earth. Elegba and Eshu are versions of the same being.

[16] Labadee is a cruise ship port and tourist centre in Haiti.

[17] T & T: Trinidad and Tobago.

[18] Boonggy: a Bahamian term for "buttocks".

[19] "Free movement of people far" alludes to the fact that The Bahamas has not signed for full accession to CARICOM. One of the clauses which have not been accepted relates to free movement of peoples among member countries for residence and work as obtains in the EC.
[20] J.C. Penney: a major US department store chain, selling mid-range clothing, favoured by many Bahamians.
[21] Mofongo: Puerto Rican dish made of fried, mashed, and seasoned green plantain.
[22] Jerk: a method of seasoning and barbecuing meats, inherited from the aboriginal inhabitants of the Caribbean, popularized by modern Jamaicans and now found throughout the Caribbean.
[23] Guava duff: a much favoured Bahamian dessert: a boiled pudding filled with strips of guava flesh and eaten with a rum-flavoured, whipped butter and sugar sauce.
[24] Junkanoo: the masquerade tradition of The Bahamas, staged most spectacularly in the early hours of Boxing Day and New Year's Day, but also used on a smaller scale to enliven other special occasions. "Cropover" is the principal festival of Barbados and "Carnival" is celebrated throughout the Lesser Antilles, especially in Trinidad & Tobago, where the tradition finds its grandest expression.
[25] "Wine down": in Caribbean Creole languages this is a dance move in which dancers, in a sensuous, sensual motion, bend the knees slowly and go as low to the floor as possible without falling. "Wine" = "wind".
[26] Pan: the steel pan, a percussion instrument developed in Trinidad and used extensively to create Carnival music. Here it means the music produced by this instrument.
[27] Goombay drum: a Bahamian round drum with a tanned goatskin drumhead. Its name is derived from that of the West African musical instrument, the *djembe*.
[28] Cowboy diplomacy: United States hegemonic interaction with the rest of the Americas and, indeed, the world.
[29] *Cocoloba uvifera.*
[30] *Chrysobalanus icaco.*
[31] "I'n" is a Bahamian Creole a compressed form for "I'm not", which is often paired, for emphasis, with another negative, such as "no", for emphasis. "I'n no civil servant" would be rendered "I'm not a civil servant" in Standard English.

[33] In the folklore of The Bahamas, the gaulin is an anthropomorphic being that exists as a great raptor bird during daylight hours and as a beautiful woman after sunset. The gaulin is identified with the Great Blue Heron (*Ardea herodias*), known for its harsh cry and fearsome display when threatened.
[34] Strega: Italian for "witch"; intended to show the sophistication of the serpent.
[35] Soucouyant: vampiric creatures, most often female, which appear in folk traditions of the Caribbean and Central and South America. In the Lesser Antilles, particularly Trinidad, the creatures are called "soucouyant". In Colombia and Ecuador, the name is "Tunda" and in The Bahamas, "hag" or "higue".
[36] Jah: an abbreviation of "Jehovah", used in the Rastafari religion to signify God.
[37] Nanny (also known as Queen Nanny or Nanny of the Maroons): a leader of the Maroons (runaway slaves who occupied the Jamaican Blue Mountains). In 1739 the British, appreciative of the Maroons' fierce fighting skills and their knowledge of the dangerous terrain, signed a treaty with the Maroons.
[38] Mary Seacole: Jamaican-born woman of colour. She set up accommodation for sick and convalescent soldiers behind the lines during the Crimean War. Known to have aided wounded soldiers on the battlefield. Forgotten for long years after her death, she was named to Jamaica's Order of Merit in 1991 and voted "greatest black Briton" in 2004.
[39] Dame Doris Johnson: was the first woman to contest an election for the Parliament of The Bahamas and the first to become a Minister of Government.
[40] Dame Eugenia Charles: first woman prime minister of Dominica and the second to lead a government in the Caribbean.
[41] Amanda Bloomer: American women's rights and temperance advocate.
[42] Sojourner Truth: born Isabella Baumfree, an African-American abolitionist and women's rights activist.
[43] Rosa Parks: African-American civil rights activist. In refusing to give up her seat on a bus to a white person, she gave great impetus to the Civil Rights Movement of the United States.

[44] Bose: Bose Corporation, founded by Indian-American Amar Bose. Manufactures high-end audio equipment.
[45] Jook (from "jook joint" or "juke joint", believed to derive from Wolof dzug, *to live wickedly*, and Bambara dzugu, *wicked*). The jook joint is Bahamian Creole for a low-class, disorderly establishment offering liquor and dance music, where drunken fights, involving "jooking" or stabbing, are likely to break out.
[47] Mazorca: Mexican term for ear of maize/corn. As used in the context of the poem, "Pelar la mazorca" ("peeling the mazorca") signifies removing the husk from an ear of corn; but the term is used familiarly to mean grinning from ear to ear. In 'Woman Unconquerable' it has connotations of forced sycophant or sexual behaviour.
[48] Kaprang: Bahamian Creole word meaning "broken down vehicle", e.g. bicycle or motorized vehicle. Used among British airmen during World War II as a verb signifying "crash".
[49] Witch of Gambaga: reference derived from the 2010 documentary directed by Yaba Badoe, a Ghanaian-British woman. The film features women who have been condemned as witches; the judgment often based on such trivial matters as whether a dying fowl expires with its wings pointed upwards or downwards. Exiled from their families and home villages, such women are forced to live in refugee towns like Gambaga in Northern Ghana, where, in return for permission to remain (although in circumstances little better than slaves), they are compelled to pay tribute to the chief.
[50] Loa, duppy, jumbie and sperrit are terms commonly used in the Caribbean region for spirits, disembodied beings, which can be good but are mostly evil and frightening. The "loa" (pronounced "lwa") are the beings in the Haitian Vodou religion who act as intermediaries between the creator and humankind. "Duppy" is common to Jamaica; "jumbie" to the lesser Antilles and "sperrit" to The Bahamas.
[51] The Pear Garden: the first known royal acting and musical academy in China. Came to be used for the world of Chinese opera in general.
[52] "Djembe": See note 27 above.

ABOUT PROVERSE HONG KONG

Proverse Hong Kong is based in Hong Kong with expanding long-term regional and international connections.

Proverse has published novels, novellas, fictionalized autobiography, non-fiction (including biography, history, memoirs, sport, travel narratives), single-author poetry collections, children's, teens / young adult and academic books. Other interests include diaries, and academic works in the humanities, social sciences, cultural studies, linguistics and education. Some Proverse books have accompanying audio texts. Some are translated into Chinese.

Proverse welcomes authors who have a story to tell, wisdom, perceptions or information to convey, a person they want to memorialize, a neglect they want to remedy, a record they want to correct, a strong interest that they want to share, skills they want to teach, and who consciously seek to make a contribution to society in an informative, interesting and well-written way. Proverse works with texts by non-native-speaker writers of English as well as by native English-speaking writers.

The name, "Proverse", combines the words "prose" and "verse" and is pronounced accordingly.

As of June 2017, Proverse administers two international prizes for literary work submitted in English.

THE PROVERSE PRIZE

The Proverse Prize, an annual international competition for an unpublished book-length work of fiction, non-fiction, or poetry, was established in January 2008. Unusually for a competition of this nature, it is open to all who are at least eighteen on the date they sign the entry form and without restriction of nationality, residence or citizenship.

The objectives of the Proverse Prize are: to encourage excellence and / or excellence and usefulness in publishable written work in the English Language, which can, in varying degrees, "delight and instruct". Entries are invited from anywhere in the world. Long-listed writers to date include writers born or resident in Andorra, Australia, Canada, Germany, Hong Kong, New Zealand, Nigeria, Singapore, Taiwan, The Bahamas, the PRC, the United Arab Emirates, the United Kingdom, the USA.

PREVIOUS WINNERS OF THE PROVERSE PRIZE

Rebecca Tomasis, for her novel, "Mishpacha – Family"
Laura Solomon, for her young adult novella,
"Instant Messages"
Gillian Jones, for her novel, "A Misted Mirror"
David Diskin, for his novel, "The Village in the Mountains"
Peter Gregoire, for his novel, "Article 109"
Sophronia Liu, for her collection of sketches,
"A Shimmering Sea"
Birgit Linder, for her illustrated poetry collection,
"Shadows in Deferment"
James McCarthy, for his biography,
"The Diplomat of Kashgar"
Philip Chatting, for "The Snow Bridge and Other Stories"
Celia Claase, for her essay and poetry collection,
"The Layers Between"
Lawrence Gray, for his novel, "Adam's Franchise"
Gustav Preller, for his novel,
"Curveball: Life never comes at you straight"

THE INTERNATIONAL PROVERSE POETRY PRIZE (SINGLE POEMS)

An annual international Proverse Poetry Prize (for single poems) was established in 2016. The international Proverse Poetry Prize is open to all who are at least eighteen years old whatever their residence, nationality or citizenship.

Single poems, submitted in English, are invited on (a) any subject or theme, chosen by the writer OR (b) on a subject or theme selected by the organizers each year.

Poems may be in any form, style or genre. Each poem should be no more than 30 lines.

Entries should previously be unpublished in any way (except in the case of unpublished translations into English of the entrant's own work already published in another language, providing the entrant holds the copyright).

In 2016, cash prizes were offered as follows:
1st prize; USD100.00; 2nd prize: USD45.00;
3rd prizes (up to four winners): USD20.00.

KEY DATES FOR THE PROVERSE POETRY PRIZE IN 2017 ONWARDS

(subject to confirmation and/or change)

Receipt of entered work, entry forms and entry fees	7 May to 30 June of the year of entry
Announcement of Winners	Before April of the year following the year of entry
Cash Awards Made	At the same time as publication of the winning poems (whether in the Proverse newsletter or website, or in an anthology) OR, if an anthology is published at the same time as the launch of the anthology at an event in Hong Kong.
Publication of an anthology of winning and other selected entries	Contingent on the quality of entries in any year

POETRY AND POETRY COLLECTIONS
Published by Proverse Hong Kong

Astra and Sebastian, by L.W. Illsley. 2011.
Bliss of Bewilderment by Birgit Bunzel Linder.2017.
Chasing light, by Patricia Glinton Meicholas. 2013.
China suite and other poems, by Gillian Bickley. 2009.
For the record and other poems of Hong Kong, by Gillian Bickley. 2003.
Frida Kahlo's Cry and Other Poems,
by Laura Solomon. 2015.
Home, away, elsewhere, by Vaughan Rapatahana. 2011.
Immortelle and bhandaaraa poems,
by Lelawattee Manoo-Rahming. 2011.
In vitro, by Laura Solomon. 2nd ed. 2014.
Irreverent Poems for Pretentious People,
by Henrik Hoeg. 2016.
Moving house and other poems from Hong Kong,
by Gillian Bickley. 2005.
Of Leaves & Ashes, by Patty Ho. 2016.
Of symbols misused, by Mary-Jane Newton. 2011.
Over the Years, by Gillian Bickley, 2017.
Painting the borrowed house: poems,
by Kate Rogers. 2008.
Perceptions, by Gillian Bickley. 2012.
Rain on the pacific coast, by Elbert Siu Ping Lee. 2013.
refrain, by Jason S. Polley. 2010.
Shadow play, by James Norcliffe. 2012.
Shadows in Deferment, by Birgit Bunzel Linder. 2013.
Shifting Sands, by Deepa Vanjani. 2016.
Sightings: a collection of poetry, with an essay, 'communicating poems', by Gillian Bickley. 2007.
Smoked pearl: poems of Hong Kong and beyond,
by Akin Jeje (Akinsola Olufemi Jeje). 2010.
The Burning Lake by Jonathan Locke Hart, 2016.
The Layers Between (Essays and Poems),
by Celia Claase. 2015.
Unlocking, by Mary-Jane Newton. March 2014.
Wonder, lust & itchy feet, by Sally Dellow. 2011.

FIND OUT MORE ABOUT OUR AUTHORS BOOKS, EVENTS AND LITERARY PRIZES

Visit our website:
http://www.proversepublishing.com

Visit our distributor's website:
<www.chineseupress.com>
Follow us on Twitter
Follow news and conversation: twitter.com/Proversebooks>
OR
Copy and paste the following to your browser window and follow the instructions:
https://twitter.com/#!/ProverseBooks
"Like" us on www.facebook.com/ProversePress

Request our free E-Newsletter
Send your request to info@proversepublishing.com.

Availability
Most titles are available in Hong Kong and world-wide from our Hong Kong based Distributor,
The Chinese University of Hong Kong Press,
The Chinese University of Hong Kong, Shatin, NT,
Hong Kong SAR, China.
Email: cup-bus@cuhk.edu.hk
Website: <www.chineseupress.com>.
All titles are available from Proverse Hong Kong
http://www.proversepublishing.com
and the Proverse Hong Kong UK-based Distributor.

We have **stock-holding retailers** in Hong Kong,
Singapore (Select Books),
Canada (Elizabeth Campbell Books),
Andorra (Llibreria La Puça, La Llibreria).
Orders can be made from bookshops in the UK and elsewhere.

Ebooks
Most of our titles are available also as Ebooks.

www.ingramcontent.com/pod-product-compliance
Lightning Source LLC
Chambersburg PA
CBHW071120160426
43196CB00013B/2641
* 9 7 8 9 8 8 8 2 2 8 1 1 9 *